ZERO BY MOSTEL

PHOTOGRAPHS BY MAX WALDMAN
WITH SOME PERSONAL WORDS
& DRAWINGS BY ZERO MOSTEL

ZERO BY MOSTEL

HORIZON PRESS NEW YORK

© 1965 by Horizon Press Publishers Ltd
Library of Congress Catalog No. 65-22556
Typography by Howard O. Bullard. Printed in
the United States of America by the Comet
Press. Bound by Publishers Book Bindery

SOME PERSONAL WORDS AND DRAWINGS

A fact that may take a certain number of years to be accepted is that Zero Mostel is secretly a very modest man.

The publishers felt that his marvelous pantomimes so beautifully photographed by Max Waldman in this book would be enhanced by Some Personal Words by Mr. Mostel; and we asked him to write an introduction. Normally most obliging to his friends, in this case he demurred for the first time. Introductions, he thought, were for egotists with overdeveloped egos.

So we asked Zero to let himself be interviewed by us. Knowing that he had submitted to innumerable interviews by professionals, we thought he would welcome the opportunity to talk for publication to a friend. He did. But he asked us first to publish his side of this history. This is what he wrote:

> I cannot gracefully write about myself. To do it seems to me like an actor whipping out a superlative review of himself (usually by a sports writer turned drama critic while the regular drama critic was out to a Mets ball game). Besides, I don't care to look back. The human history is not so hot. I hate to write. But my editor Ben Raeburn is my old friend. He is doing a book about me, despite my graceful objections, and he asked me whether I would like to write an introduction. I don't care for introductions. Ben is my friend. I love him. So we decided on an alternative and I answered a few of his questions.

Thus Zero.

The conversations took place in a variety of circumstances: at lunches, in restaurants where our talks were punctually interrupted by other diners and waiters asking him to autograph menus, napkins, cards, anything loose and portable; during walks around New York streets, where the same kind of interruptions inevitably

occurred; then in his downtown studio, where we sat, secluded at last, before a large electric fan amidst canvases, pencils, easels, drawings, tables, piles of paint tubes, brushes, an etching press, art books, sculptures by Herb Kallem, reproductions, watercolors — in a clutter that discloses the wonderful natural order of the working artist's privacy. It is in this room that this colossally gifted man finds seclusion from the adulation and exposure of the theatre, revealing another side of his genius in a massive flow of paintings and drawings, astonishing in their vitality, their imaginative, searching experiment, and inventive skill. (Even here, a telephone, private, unlisted, unknown, rang continuously); then in his dressing room backstage, filled with works of art and drawings done by his sons Joshua and Tobias, and here visitors from all the earth's corners came in and went out with weird regularity as if rooted on a treadmill; and finally in his uptown apartment, a personal

museum whose walls are covered with paintings, etchings, lithographs, collages, drawings, by Klee, Picasso, Rembrandt, Renoir, Léger, Pascin, Tatti, Joe di Martinis, A. Birnbaum, Henry Kallem, Nick Luisi, Ralph Rosenborg, Henry Rothman, and Zero Mostel; illuminated manuscripts; magnificent weavings, glass-framed, of

Peruvian, Arabian and Coptic cloth; luminous cabinets of antiquities and Pre-Columbian art, an incomparable collection; bookcases full of art books, fiction, biography, drama, in English, French, German, Yiddish, Italian — all of which he reads. There is a violin, played by Joshua; and there are two grand pianos, played both by

Tobias and by Zero's wife Kate, who is the possessor of a flashing, hilarious wit and of its counterpart, a quick and sympathetic perceptivity.

A man in whom the generosities and faiths of friendship spring in constant impulses, a host whose thoughtfulness runs deep, Zero Mostel invariably generates an atmosphere of warmth and welcome. In this sentient air, talk and listening are spontaneous pleasures.

His wit as always a radiance about him, readily articulate and reflective, his thought enlarged by manifold experience — in the theatre, in films, before his easel, in his impatient travels to see paintings he loves in the museums of Europe, in his reading of the world's good books — Zero responded beautifully.

Had space permitted, we would gladly have had many more pages of these conversations:

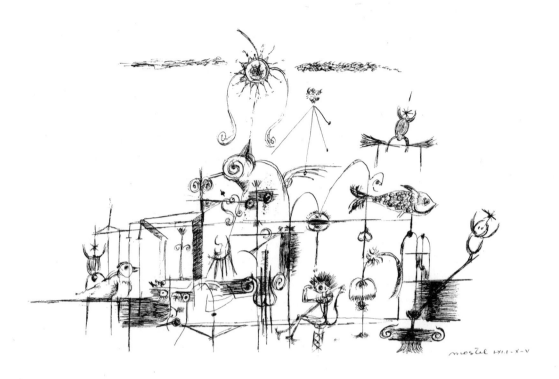

How did you get on the stage?

Ben, I just don't know how to answer that. I was analyzed for years of my adult life and I never did find out why I gravitated toward the stage. A significant clue might be in this: My poor mother wanted me to be a rabbi. But then, she was always a great wit.

Why do you both paint and act?

It is a better combination than assault and battery, or true and blue, or nook and cranny. I feel there are too many hours in the day. But I really don't know why I paint and act; what I do know is that if I didn't I would be very unhappy.

Do you think acting is important?

Acting is important when you are in a play that makes people feel or enlightens people or elates people or cerebrates people or celebrates people.

Do you think painting is important?

I'd like to answer that in two parts: Part 1: Is *my* painting important? To me it is. Part 2: Is painting important? To me it is.

But the word "important" is obscure to me because I don't know its value. What I can tell you is that some paintings give me a feeling of serenity or cause a happy turmoil, some lead me into a maze of wonderings, some excite me. The thing that always fascinates me is what the human hand can accomplish.

In working out a part when do you sense that it is right?

I feel it's right if my own inner censor knows what I am doing. Sometimes your intuition tells you certain things: to speak faster, or to speak more slowly, or to be less or more graceful. I think it's a matter of innate taste and intuition, much the same as in drawing or painting. When I draw, I often feel that not everything I see with the naked eye may be quite right for a particular drawing. In the same way, if I know the life of the character I am doing, I can use my inventiveness to eliminate or supplement an element of the character, and so create a spontaneity every night, every performance.

Hemingway said that if you omit what you know it is still there and the quality of the work will show, but if you omit what you don't know it leaves a hole in your work.

Actors who get so involved with the character that they live with it all the time, both on *and* off the stage and want to show it, tend to take the mundane, trivial things about it and play those things solely, but in that way they never expose the truth of the character.

When I was playing an adaptation of *Malade Imaginaire*, I was puzzled by a line I had written myself. Frankly, I didn't know what it meant. The director, a very pompous individual, said to me: "I know what's troubling you, Zero" [using my first name — a breach of our uncordial relationship]. And he went on: "Play the first part of the line with half volume in your voice. Cackle. Pause. And then play the rest of the line with a gleam of ferocity in your eyes."

I said to him: "Mr. Director, you've solved my problem . . . But I still don't know what the line means."

Those are some of the trivia with which a helpful director assassinates the truth of a character.

As you go from portraying one character to another, do you learn much from experience?

Yes, you do learn from experience but it is important not to have a pedagogical approach to the character. Many people who

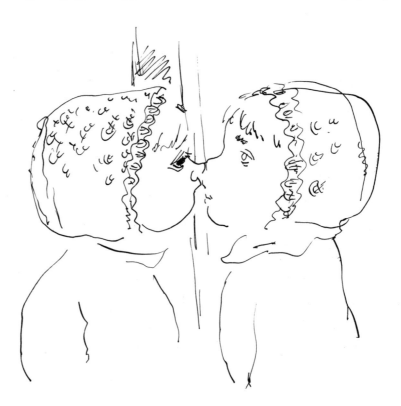

work in the theatre say "if you train your intuition, you'll know more" but if the performance is approached with pedagogical ideas it will fail. The problem is always one of keeping a play fresh; and what does that is the way you are, the way you feel, see, think; and your awareness of the environment, of heat and cold, of the life around you. You have to be aware of your senses. It is some sort of mania that possesses you, something like a catatonic state, and a good director understands that that is how you keep a play fresh. Of course, an asinine director will try to spoil it for you.

There is another aspect of experience. If an actor says: "I'm getting much better" and if that is the thing that he is concerned with, he eliminates and wastes his resources; like the painter who says "I paint in this way, or that way." What is important, when you look at a painting, is: Here — this is the painting, that's the artist who painted it.

Let someone else say you are great. Don't be aware of greatness. Just do your job. And be critical of your function, of the way in which you do it, instead of wondering how good you are. And so with acting. If you are re-creating the part fresh every night, it won't have much to do with learning from experience or progress or the past. An actor is faced with doing his job every day and he should take a chance with his taste. At best he can say,

I think I was good in this, and he can feel that doing a good job is enough for him, rather than have any sense of being great.

Luckily you can't see yourself. Nor do you want to. Nor is it necessary. I think the artist, in any field, is concerned in the *act* of creation, not in the *result* of creation.

How do you go about preparing a new role after you first see the script?

I do push-ups. Actually I barely do one push-up. Having thus exercised, I try everything. I go wild, or I try it with complete restraint, I supplement, eliminate, I shout, then whisper the part, then relate it to everyone else in the play. I listen to what the other characters say, I re-shape what I say to them. There comes a time when the inner censor says: You are speaking the truth; now you know the essence of the character.

I am often told about how well I ad lib on the stage but it is not ad libbing. People tend to mistake spontaneity for ad libbing. You know that a good pianist, each time he has to play the same Mozart sonata, has to re-create it entirely, within the limits of the music. He is not a metronome. An actor does not have complete freedom either; he doesn't change a line in a play at his whim. But faced with re-creating a part every night, he must employ his imagination every night. He should feel every night that he is telling the truth.

If a good actor gets involved in a poor play, how does he manage to do that every night? Is it possible to take bad lines that seem untrue to you in speaking them and make good lines of them?

The actor has a specific problem, and a responsibility. Once you have agreed to do it, you have to do it, you do all you can to make it a true thing. And once you are in, you accept the fact that you are in for a long time, and each time you do it with everything you have. The good Lord who has compassion even for good actors may deliver you some day.

Which actors have you thought most highly of?

There are many good ones, but few great. Chaplin is one.

Why?

Of course we have never seen him on the stage, but in everything he has done in the films you are always aware of his tremendous imagination, his artistry, his sympathy, and that marvelous natural grace of his.

Who else?

Raimu. In his every performance, you always felt that whatever character he created he seemed to have lifted out of the abyss of humanity and made it a symbol of meaning for all men. And through the distortion that he brought to his portrayals, you felt he gave them the proper proportions and as a result they possessed a great truth.

Laurette Taylor was another great one; in her *mis*-accenting of words, in the slurring over of words apparently as though they had no meaning, in her pauses — I am speaking of her performance in *The Glass Menagerie* — you felt that by that same means of imaginative distortion she had created a great and rounded character.

Charles Laughton was another, but he was a very different case. You saw his knowledge at work, you were always aware of it. He was perhaps not as profoundly equipped as Raimu, but there was something about the restraint with which he worked that was very effective and moving.

What movies have meant a great deal to you?

    The Baker's Wife with Raimu — Chaplin's *The Gold Rush* —
W. C. Fields, in anything.

And plays?

    I think I have been moved more by performers than by plays.
Laurette Taylor, as I have said, in *The Glass Menagerie*, Brando
in *Streetcar*, Olivier in *Oedipus*, Meredith in *Candida*, Jaffe in
Grand Hotel. When you see a great one, you are never the same.

*What about those great performances of yours? Jean in Rhinoc-
eros, Bloom in Ulysses, Tevye in Fiddler, the others?*

    I don't know what to say about them. I didn't see them.

What do you think about publicity for the actor?

I think it's unfortunate. It would be wonderful if one could be judged just by his ability, preferably unspoken. And if his private life were left to himself he could prepare himself solely to perfect the work he's engaged in. I dislike having my photograph in a restaurant, with an insipid inscription to the owner. If I were someone else gazing at my photograph, it would spoil my digestion.

There is always the platitude about an actor's most rewarding role; have you felt any such thing?

I've taken equal pleasure in most of the parts: Bloom in *Ulysses*, Jean in *Rhinoceros*, even Pseudolus in *A Funny Thing Happened on the Way to the Forum*, of course Tevye in *Fiddler*, and in some of the night club work: the Senator, the pantomime of the coffee percolator (it always used to amaze me when they laughed), the piece about Mother; and I had great pleasure in doing Moliere, the *Malade Imaginaire*, in the Brattle Theatre in Cambridge.

Did your playing of those characters change much during the long runs?

Once I'm on the stage in a part I am always in the process of freshening it and keeping it spontaneous. If audiences feel that what they are seeing is being done for the first time, I am happy. Not that I speak to all of them after a performance — but one can feel, can't he?

Are there any parts you would like to do again?

I would like to do Bloom in *Ulysses* again.

Why?

I just love its elegant inventive language. It is the father of

all modern plays. Many a penpusher has dipped his nose into that great master's ink.

And I often think of doing *Waiting for Godot* again. I believe it to be a classic of our time. Beckett reflects the modern world for everyone who is willing to see it with a clear mind, purged of preconceptions; he presents the dilemmas of modern life; his play is the work of an artist.

People often say about these two great plays that they "mean nothing" but even the fact that they "mean nothing" is marvelous. Really they mean a great deal, the *mystère* of life is in these works.

What does Cézanne's Mont St. Victoire "mean?" What does a mountain mean? As seen through an artist's eyes it is a fantastic wonder to behold. How he saw that mountain! And how, therefore, we can now see that mountain. When I first saw the painting, though I had never seen it before, I nevertheless felt somehow that it had existed. It was actually as if a dream came true, yet I had never had that dream, or seen that mountain, or that painting.

That's *mystère*. That painting is one of the highest aspirations of man in our history. Would you believe I have heard people say it's overpriced, at $750,000? Yet nobody says that about the billions we spend for bombs. I wish I could reverse the values. Less dreadnoughts, more painting.

Shaw says in *Don Juan* that we have mastered only the arts of warfare — yes, it has been mastered by the idiots that want it — yet the Minoan sculpture will outlast wars and survive. The shape of something beautiful, a Minoan vase or a matriarchal figure of Greek civilization, such things are the best we have.

(At this point we stopped. It was Saturday evening. We had worked together all day.)

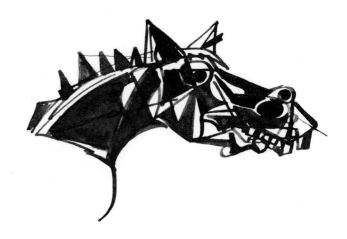

It is Sunday morning. The publisher's telephone rings. It is Zero. The voice is low, almost a whisper, conspiratorial. He asks:

"Did I wake you?"

"No."

"Then go back to sleep and I'll call you."

"Good."

Long pause. Again Zero whispers:

"Would you like to work today?"

"What time?"

"One."

"No."

"One-ten?"

"No."

"One-four?"

"No."

"When?"

"One."

"O.K. Think it over and call me Tuesday."

It is Monday. We are back in Zero's study. He says:

"You know, I have a fantasy about the painting of the Rabbi by Rembrandt in The National Gallery in London — that it knows it is good. Whenever I come back to see it, it seems to me that the Rabbi says: Where were you? I am overjoyed that you are here. And I say to him: How is your lot? And he says: The same.

I feel about him as I do for a lost old friend whom I may not have seen for years. But he is always there. He looks at me and I look at him, and I'm sorry I have to leave. I think the old Rabbi also looks sad.

Have accidents on the stage given you any problems?

Very often. But you take it in your stride, and you do the best you can. Once in *Fiddler*, the house, which was supposed to move in a certain way, went every which way. So, in one of my colloquies with God, I said to Him "Just because I didn't pay the rent to the landlord, you don't have to punish me." And when the stage hands worked feverishly to put the house in the proper place, which took quite some time, I said "If you were a decent God, you'd put my house in order." And God, in the form of a stage hand, did.

Do you read your reviews?

I read them but I hope I am not influenced by them, whether good or bad. If an actor feels he is doing a good job, doing the meaning of the role for the public, he should feel secure despite what anybody may say.

I once got awful reviews in a play but well-wishers called to say how terrible the reviews were and how unfair the critics, and under the circumstances I felt I could do no better. The play didn't last and I had more time to paint for awhile. But I managed to survive.

How long have you been painting?

I've been cursed since the age of nine. When I was a child,

I drew everything I saw exactly as it was. I drew my father, and my mother said: "Look at him. A child — and he draws like a man."

When I was twenty she saw an abstract work I did. And she said: "Look at him. A grown man — and he draws like a child."

May I see your drawings of your father?

Yes. Here are some I did when I was thirteen.

Do you know what first interested you in painting?

No one has yet successfully explained why primitive man had to decorate his pot or what painting means or what it does

for you. From the first moment that I found I could manipulate paint, I was in love with it — or with looking at someone else's paintings. I don't really know whether I enjoy looking or painting better. I'm happy with both.

In your painting you experiment constantly in a variety of mediums.

I know that there are artists who figure out a palette, and are concerned with the Big Meaning and with philosophies of painting, etc., but a way of painting is great because of the *artist* who did it. Painting need not be done in any one way. It seems to me that trying a variety of ways, and a variety of mediums, keeps the mentality fresh. I've heard it said that Cézanne stopped experimenting, but I don't believe it, somehow he is different in every one of his paintings. And there is often much talk about an artist's painting being like this or that or the other painter. I see nothing wrong with that. People seem to be afraid to let things rub off. After all, in the end you take it out of your own hand, your own way of seeing; there is really nothing new but you use it for *yourself*. Anyway, it is better to derive from Cézanne than from Maxfield Parrish. Was it Eliot who said: "Bad poets imitate, good poets steal"? Yes, it was Eliot.

What paintings have meant most to you?

There is "The Garden of Delights" by Bosch in the Prado. There are times when I have felt that I could sink into that painting and stay there the rest of my life. I was so happy to see that painting and I am aching to see it again.

There is the "Flemish Proverbs" by Breughel. There are Rembrandt's "Susanna and The Elders," "The Rabbi," and the last self-portrait, the one in the Mauritz House in The Hague, a painting done in thick brush strokes and probably very fast, with the spontaneous assurance of a master, and startling color as if it had been poured out. It made me weep.

There is also the wonderful "Saul and David" of Rembrandt in the Mauritz House. And Botticelli's "Birth of Venus" — I could die happily looking at that one; and the color world of any of Klee's; the world of Cézanne; of da Vinci. And I love the analytical, clear world of Vermeer in his "View of Delft"; da Vinci's unfinished Saint Jerome is a marvelous painting. I enjoy the mentality of Picasso. I admire Delacroix's "Corner of the Studio" and Daumier's "Third Class Carriage"; I like Ensor; I enjoy the way Kokoschka explores life with his hot high color. In fact I love any good painting — any except the commercial nonentities that we have too damn much of everywhere.

What about architecture? Has the kind of theatre you have played in ever made any difference?

No, it has never made any difference. But I do resent it when architects make antiseptic buildings for theatres. I'd like to see the use of architecture and art, not just builders, plumbers, and wall-paperers. And I resent it when they make parking lots or television studios out of theatres. You can't see the theatre at its best on television. Television is very good in presenting the spontaneity of sports and of current events, which is what it should do, without of course interfering with people's privacy. And it should stay away from the Shakespeare play, they just wreck it as the movies have wrecked Shakespeare. And I think all the technical things in the theatre are overrated; the design, the lighting, the sound — the technicalities. If there were no money for these things, and just a few bed sheets for the sets it would be a great boon and we would see the *play*. Notice that Shakespeare never had elaborate descriptions of the sets, but the experts drown plays with magic lanterns and colors; they concern themselves with tinsel rather than meaning. The non-creative man likes to intrude on a work of art, with phony lighting, indirect, overdirect, underdirect. And as for credits, I like a big work of art and a tiny signature.

2·19·58

Is your performance of a role ever affected by the response of an audience?

I think I am the kind of actor who doesn't concern himself with the audience. (Not that I don't like to have them around.) You just have to try to retain your own imagination and spontaneity. There are times when I have said to myself: "Are they dumb out there? They didn't get it." But then I may have been speaking too fast or my diction may not have been clear — but it is best not to be overly concerned about the audience. Audiences vary but *you* can't vary. You have to play the meaning of the play, and the kind of audience doesn't matter.

Of course, sometimes you get what seems a cold audience and with a performance you win them over and you have a good feeling about that, but the idea is to play the play, and think of nothing else. If you should think of doing what the audience would like, you could put the worst dribble on the stage; on the other hand if you should think of pleasing the intellectual snobs in the audience you could do a disservice to the play. You simply do the play according to your best understanding and keep it fresh and spontaneous; not like the actors who, because they employ some confining method of acting, are never aware of others in the cast or of the meaning of the play.

Clarity is the most important thing. Regardless of the kind of audience, they hear what you are saying and they see what you are doing and they know what you are thinking. Of course, the actor should be involved in the truth of the character, but what the actor says, does and thinks should be heard, seen and felt up to the last row in the balcony and a bit beyond, for the spectator pays a harsh tariff, so let him, for God's sake, enjoy. And abolish the electronic microphone. There is no nuance of interpretation with these mechanical gadgets. There is great beauty in the unadorned power of the actor who knows exactly what he is doing.

"Great beauty in the unadorned power of the actor who knows exactly what he is doing" — a perfectly accurate description of the events caught in the pages of this book.

The word "genius" has been used to describe Zero Mostel by critics of diverse character — Irving Howe, V. S. Pritchett, Harold Rosenberg, many others. To have the singular fortune to see genius in the act of creating itself is a profoundly enlightening experience, an ever-renewing sense of the unbounded potentialities of the human animal. To see it, moreover, wildly infused by the comic spirit — subtle or broad, always at play — is visual joy well beyond verbal reach.

That Zero Mostel's incomparably inspired pantomime should have been so magically sustained by Max Waldman's camera is miracle enough.

THE PHOTOGRAPHS

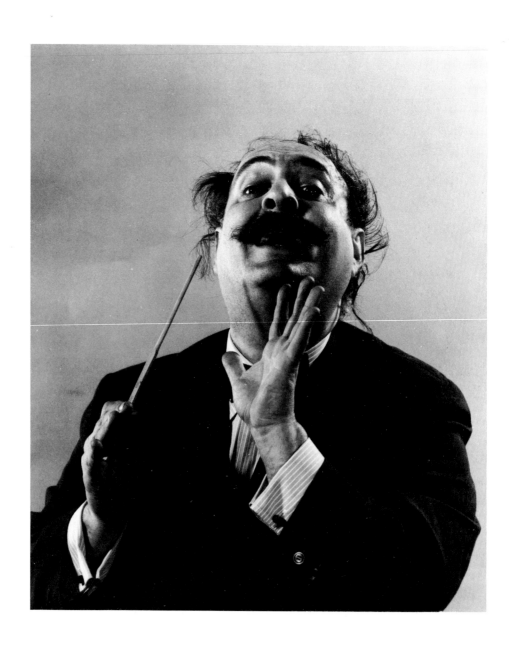

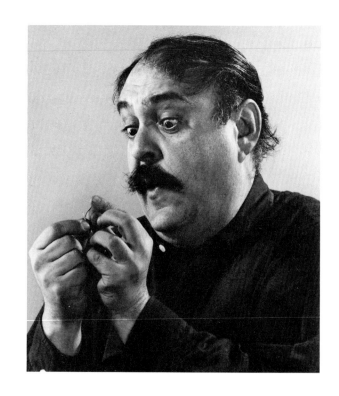

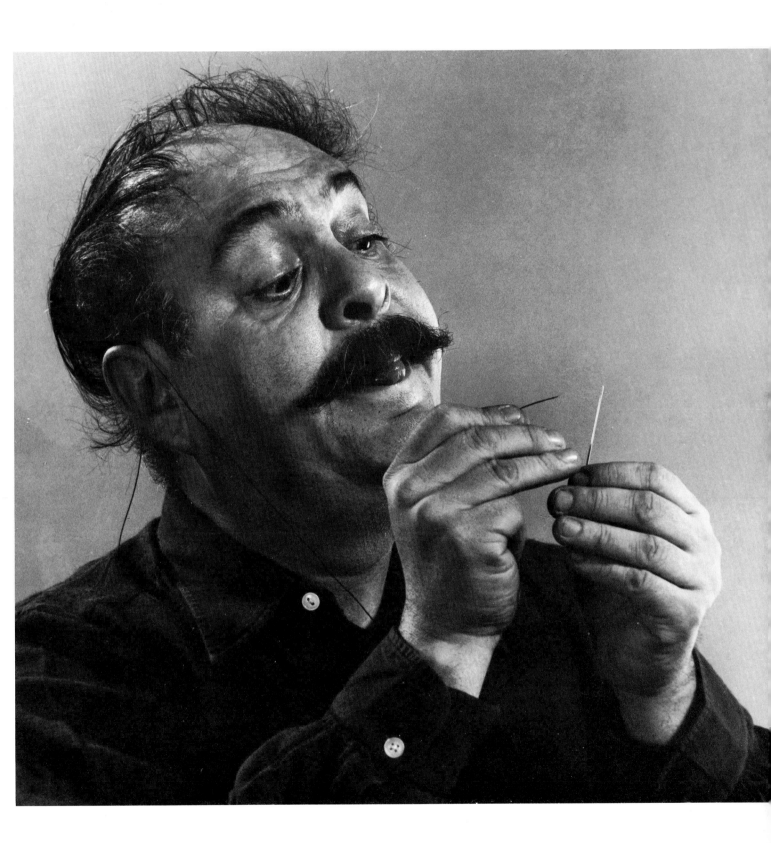

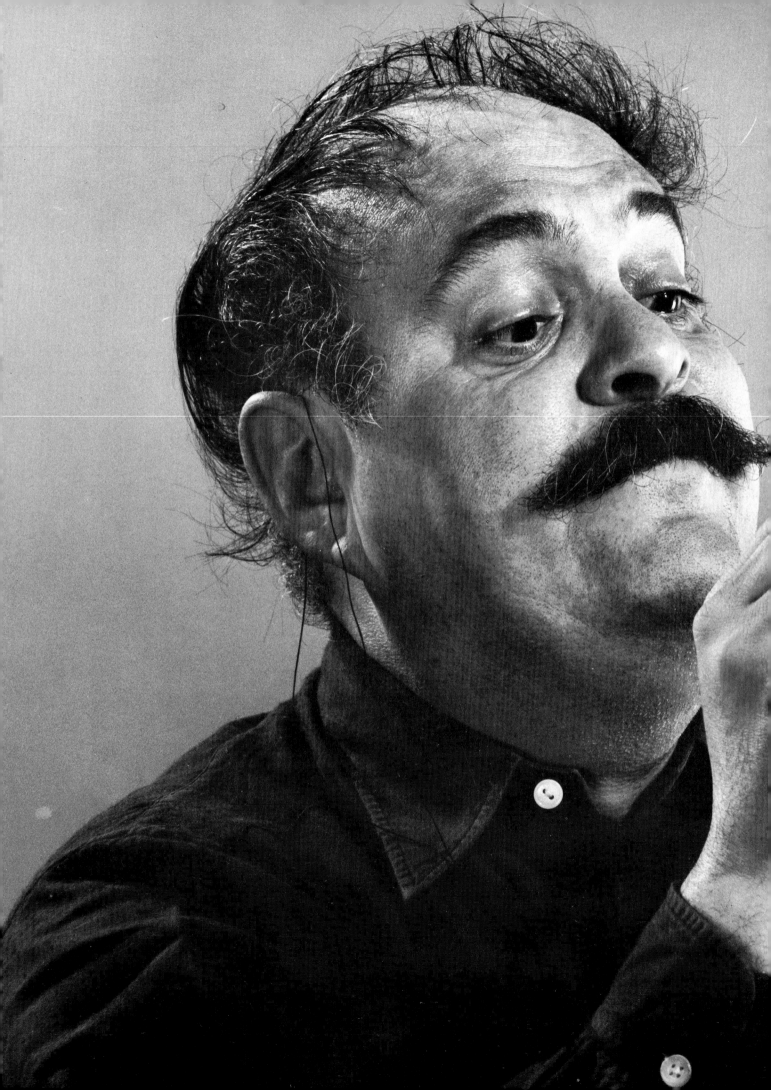

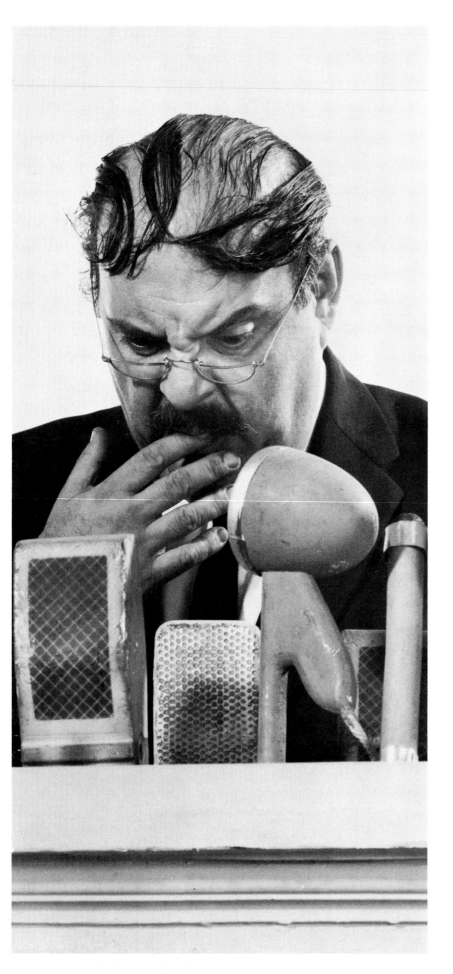

AS BLOOM IN ULYSSES IN NIGHTTOWN

AS JEAN IN RHINOCEROS

AS TEVYE IN FIDDLER ON THE ROOF